GW00363552

Peace

BOOKS
TO GO

Peace

PEACE
A New Internationalist BOOK TO GO

Published by New Internationalist Publications Ltd
55 Rectory Road
Oxford OX4 1BW
www.newint.org
New Internationalist is a registered trademark

Cover image by Paul Lowe/Panos.
Credits for other images on Page 190.

© New Internationalist 2005

Compiled by Dinyar Godrej.

Designed/Edited by Alan Hughes/Chris Brazier.

Printed on recycled paper by South China Printing Co Ltd,
Hong Kong, China.

British Library Cataloguing-in-Publication Data.
A catalogue record for this book is available from the British Library.

ISBN 1 904456 23 5

Introduction

NO PEACE IS TO be had without first
staring down a demon. You have to
face the stress in order to soothe.

That is why this little book keeps its
distance from the wishy-washy and
the woolly. Instead its visionary words
grapple squarely with the problems
of violence and division that must be
resolved before the banner of peace
can fly free.

Little can change in our world without
the exercise of power of one sort or

5

another. Politicians know this only too well, but their view of power tends to be largely coercive. Hundreds of millions of ordinary citizens know otherwise. They would rather exert the greater power of peace, however difficult it might be to achieve.

Dinyar Godrej

Note: old quotations using 'man' as a generic term for all people have generally been adapted to accord with modern usage.

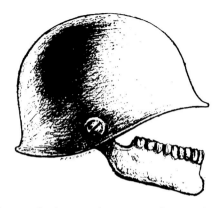

I like to believe that people in the
long run are going to do more to
promote peace than our governments.
Indeed, I think that people want
peace so much that one of these days
governments had better get out of the
way and let them have it.

Dwight D Eisenhower (1890-1969), US President and General

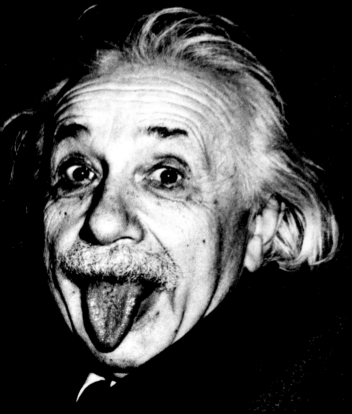

I am an absolute pacifist... It is an instinctive feeling. It is a feeling that possesses me, because the murder of men is disgusting.

Albert Einstein (1879-1955), scientist, pictured left on his 72nd birthday in 1951

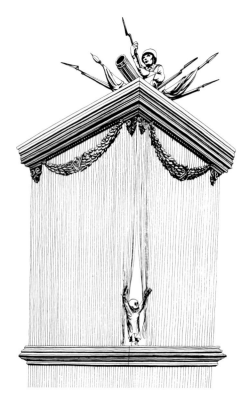

10

HAVE WE NOT come to such an impasse in the modern world that we must love our enemies – or else? The chain reaction of evil – hate begetting hate, wars producing more wars – must be broken, or else we shall be plunged into the dark abyss of annihilation.

Martin Luther King Jr (1929-1968), African-American civil rights leader

12

I spent 33 years and four months in active service as a member of our country's most agile military force – the Marine Corps. I served in all commissioned ranks from Second Lieutenant to Major-General. And during that time I spent most of my time being a high-class muscle man for Big Business, for Wall Street and for the bankers. In short, I was a racketeer for capitalism.

Smedley E Butler, US general, speaking in 1935. He is pictured at a rally in Philadelphia the same year.

13

14

Peace be to the Earth and to the Air! Peace be to Heaven, peace to the Waters! By this invocation of peace may peace bring peace.

Atharva Veda, Hindu scriptures (1500-800 BCE)

THE BIRDS WERE
the things we could
see all the time. They
were superb specimens
of life... really quite
exquisite... phenomenal
creatures. Albatrosses
will fly for days, skimming
a few inches above the
surface of the water. These birds
have tremendously long wings
and tails... Watching them is a
wonder...

They were now suddenly visible
through the opaque visor of my
helmet. And they were smoking.

16

Their feathers were on fire. And they were doing cartwheels... They were sizzling, smoking... absorbing such intense radiation that they were being consumed by the heat. Their feathers were on fire. They were blinded. And so far there had been no shock, none of the blast damage we talk about when we discuss the effects of nuclear weapons. Instead there were just those smoking, twisting, hideously contorted birds crashing into things.

An observer of a US atomic bomb test at Christmas Island in the Pacific

Not HAMMER STROKES, BUT DANCE OF THE WATER SINGS THE PEBBLES INTO PERFECTION.

Rabindranath Tagore (1861-1941), Bengali poet and philosopher

ONCE PEOPLE UNDERSTAND THE STRENGTH OF NON-VIOLENCE – THE FORCE IT GENERATES, THE LOVE IT CREATES, THE RESPONSE IT BRINGS FROM THE TOTAL COMMUNITY – THEY WILL NOT EASILY ABANDON IT.

Cesar Chavez (1927-1993),
Mexican-American labour activist

There's a consensus out that it's OK to kill when your government decides who to kill. If you kill inside the country you get in trouble. If you kill outside the country, right time, right season, latest enemy, you get a medal.

Joan Baez (1941-), US folk singer and activist, pictured at a 1975 concert in Central Park, New York, to celebrate the end of the US-Vietnam War

22

Graffito magazine, March 1977

23

WE DROWSE OUR
WAY TOWARDS THE
END OF THE WORLD

IF WE COULD LEARN TO LOVE, THEN WAR WOULD BE IMPOSSIBLE, DEFENCES, BOMB-PROOF SHELTERS, ANTI-AIRCRAFT GUNS, ARMAMENTS, TREATIES A RIDICULOUS MOCKERY, THE PARAPHERNALIA OF FEAR WE HAD OUTGROWN.

Dick Sheppard (1880-1937),
founder of the Peace Pledge Union

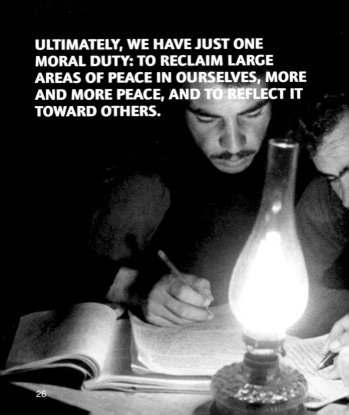

ULTIMATELY, WE HAVE JUST ONE MORAL DUTY: TO RECLAIM LARGE AREAS OF PEACE IN OURSELVES, MORE AND MORE PEACE, AND TO REFLECT IT TOWARD OTHERS.

26

AND THE MORE PEACE THERE IS IN US, THE MORE PEACE THERE WILL BE IN OUR TROUBLED WORLD.

Etty Hillesum (1914-1943), German-Jewish mystic, writer, Auschwitz victim

28

**THOUSANDS OF YEARS OF
LOVING, FAILING, KILLING,
CREATING, SURPRISING,
OPPRESSING,
AND THINKING OUGHT NOW
TO START
TO BEAR FRUIT, TO DELIVER
THEIR RICH HARVEST.**

**WILL YOU BE AT THE
HARVEST,
AMONG THE GATHERERS OF
NEW FRUITS?
THEN YOU MUST BEGIN
TODAY TO REMAKE
YOUR MENTAL AND SPIRITUAL
WORLD.**

Ben Okri (1959-), Nigerian-born poet and author

COSTS
Cost to date to the US alone of the Iraq war 2003-2004:
$155 BILLION

BENEFITS
?

COSTS

Estimated annual cost to the world of meeting the Millennium Development Goals (MDGs): $135 BILLION

BENEFITS

If the MDGs were met, in the year 2015 there would be: 504 million fewer people living in poverty; 300 million fewer suffering from malnourishment; 5.4 million children's lives saved; 390,000 mothers' lives saved in childbirth; 350 million fewer people without access to safe water; 650 million fewer people with no access to sanitation; less than half the number of new HIV infections.

Source: UNDP

Arms traders displaying their wares.

My dynamite will sooner lead to peace
Than a thousand world conventions.
As soon as men will find that in one instant
Whole armies can be utterly destroyed,
They will surely abide by golden peace.

Alfred Nobel (1833-96), inventor of dynamite and founder of the Nobel Peace Prize

After a lifetime of war-watching, I see war as an endemic human disease, and governments the carriers.

Martha Gellhorn (1908-1998), US journalist and author

A 'just war' is hospitable to every self-deception on the part of those waging it, none more than the certainty of virtue, under whose shelter every abomination can be committed with a clear conscience.

Alexander Cockburn (1941-), Anglo-Irish journalist

Non-violence is the first article of my faith. It is also the last article of my creed.

Mohandas Karamchand Gandhi (1869-1948), leader of India's freedom movement, pictured in 1941

They who do not find
peace at home are
already at war.

Arabic

'I challenge you to a duel.'
'I challenge you to go in
peace.'

Arabic

In peace time
they bury us old,
in war they bury
them young.

Arabic

'Peace upon earth!' was said.
We sing it,
And pay a million priests to bring it.
After two thousand years of mass
We've got as far as poison-gas.

Thomas Hardy (1840-1928), English
novelist and poet, from 'Christmas: 1924'

EVERY GUN THAT IS MADE, every warship launched, every rocket fired signifies, in the final sense, a theft from those who hunger and are not fed, those who are cold and are not clothed. This world in arms is not spending money alone. It is spending the sweat of labourers, the genius of scientists, the hopes of its children. The cost of one modern heavy bomber is this: a modern brick school in more than 30 cities. It is two electric power plants, each serving a town of

60,000. It is two fine, fully equipped hospitals. It is some 50 miles of concrete highway. We pay for a single destroyer with new homes that could have housed more than 8,000 people.

This, I repeat, is the best way of life to be found on the road the world has been taking.

This is not a way of life at all, in any true sense. Under the cloud threatening war, it is humanity hanging from a cross of iron.

Dwight D Eisenhower (1890-1969), US President and General

Militarism is the characteristic, not of an army, but of a society

RH Tawney
(1880-1962),
Indian-born
British socialist
thinker

ALTHOUGH MY MOTHER is often described as a political dissident who strives by peaceful means for democratic change, we should remember that her quest is basically spiritual. As she has said: 'The quintessential revolution is that of the spirit,' and she has written of the 'essential spiritual aims' of the struggle. The realization of this depends solely on human responsibility. At the root of that responsibility lies, and I quote, 'the concept of perfection, the urge to achieve it, the intelligence to find a path towards it, and the will to follow that path if not to the end, at least the distance needed to rise above individual limitation...'

Alexander Aris, delivering the 1991 Nobel Peace Prize acceptance speech for his mother, Aung San Suu Kyi (1945-), leader of the movement for democracy in Burma, who is pictured left

GRANDFATHER
LOOK AT OUR BROKENNESS,
WE KNOW THAT IN ALL CREATION
ONLY THE HUMAN FAMILY
HAS STRAYED AWAY FROM THE SACRED WAY.
WE KNOW WE ARE THE ONES
WHO ARE DIVIDED.
AND WE ARE THE ONES
WHO MUST COME BACK TOGETHER
TO WALK IN THE SACRED WAY.
GRANDFATHER, SACRED ONE,
TEACH US LOVE, COMPASSION AND HONOUR
THAT WE MAY HEAL THE EARTH
AND HEAL EACH OTHER.

Song of the Ojibway nation, Canada

*before we weave an
autumn for tyrants
we must cross this galaxy
of barbed wires
and keep on repeating
HAPPY NEW WAR*

Sinan Antoon (1967-), Iraqi poet, from the poem
'A Prism: Wet With Wars', Baghdad, March 1991

A British soldier patrolling Basra Bridge, Iraq, in 2003.

52

We test and then they test and we have to test again. And you build up until somebody uses them.

John F Kennedy (1917-1963),
US President, on nuclear testing

Bullets cannot be recalled. They cannot be uninvented. But they can be taken out of the gun.

Martin Amis (1949-), British author

Celebrations in Kenya.

What if someone gave a war and Nobody came?
Life would ring the bells of Ecstasy and Forever be Itself again.

Allen Ginsberg (1926-1997), US poet

55

IT IS SAID that in the Babemba tribe of South Africa, when a person acts irresponsibly or unjustly, he is placed in the centre of the village, alone and unfettered.

All work ceases, and every man, woman and child in the village gathers in a large circle around the accused individual. Then each person in the tribe speaks to the accused, one at a time, about all the good things the person in the centre of the circle has done in his lifetime. Every incident, every experience that can be recalled with any detail and accuracy is recounted. All his positive attributes, good deeds, strengths and kindnesses are recited carefully and at length.

The tribal ceremony often lasts several days. At the end, the tribal circle is broken, a joyous celebration takes place, and the person is symbolically and literally welcomed back into the tribe...

Alice Walker (1944-), African-American writer

The atomic bomb explosion at Hiroshima on 6 August 1945, seen from the ground.

THAT EVEN AN APOCALYPSE CAN BE MADE TO SEEM PART OF THE ORDINARY HORIZON OF EXPECTATION CONSTITUTES AN UNPARALLELED VIOLENCE THAT IS BEING DONE TO OUR SENSE OF REALITY, TO OUR HUMANITY.

Susan Sontag (1933-2004), US essayist,
on nuclear war

Between 1996 and 2000 the world's top four suppliers of major conventional weapons, in terms of total value, were:

- **UNITED STATES $49 BILLION**
- **RUSSIA $16 BILLION**
- **FRANCE $11 BILLION**
- **BRITAIN $7 BILLION**

Together with China ($2 billion) these are the five permanent members of the UN Security Council.

Source: Gideon Burrows, *No Nonsense Guide to the Arms Trade* (Verso/New Internationalist, 2002).

6

Greenham Common women's peace camp, England, 1982

The point of non-violence is to build a floor, a strong new floor, beneath which we can no longer sink. A platform which stands a few feet above napalm, torture, exploitation, poison gas, A and H bombs, the works. Give humans a decent place to stand.

Joan Baez (1941-), US folk singer and activist

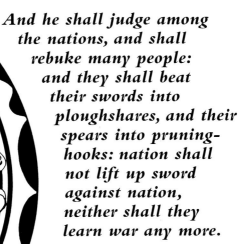

*And he shall judge among
the nations, and shall
rebuke many people:
and they shall beat
their swords into
ploughshares, and their
spears into pruning-
hooks: nation shall
not lift up sword
against nation,
neither shall they
learn war any more.*

Bible: Isaiah 2:4

LOVE'S CONQUEROR IS HE WHOM LOVE CONQUERS.

Hakim Abu'L-Majd Majdud Sanai of Ghazna (12th century), Afghan Sufi philosopher

I'VE SEEN TOO MUCH HATE to want to hate, myself, and I've seen hate on the faces of too many white sheriffs, too many white citizens' councillors, and too many Klansmen of the South to want to hate, myself; and every time I see it, I say to myself, hate is too great a burden to bear. Somehow we must be able to stand up before our most bitter opponents and say: 'We shall match your capacity to inflict suffering by our capacity to endure suffering. We will meet your physical force with soul force. Do to us what you will and we will still love you.'

Martin Luther King Jr (1929-1968), African-American leader, photographed left in 1965

Peace has never come from dropping bombs.

Real peace comes from enlightenment and educating people to behave more in a divine manner.

Carlos Santana (1947-),
Mexican-American musician

70

IT IS SAID THAT OUR INDIGENOUS ANCESTORS, MAYAS AND AZTECS, MADE HUMAN SACRIFICES TO THEIR GODS. IT OCCURS TO ME TO ASK: HOW MANY HUMANS HAVE BEEN SACRIFICED TO THE GODS OF CAPITAL IN THE LAST 500 YEARS?

Rigoberta Menchú Tum (1959-), Guatemalan activist for indigenous rights, and Nobel Peace Prize winner, 1992

War is capitalism with the gloves off.

Tom Stoppard (1937-), Czech-born British dramatist

NO WAR, not even to punish an aggressor, is a good thing. Today people must learn to take into account each others' interests, if only for the sake of their own survival. I do not believe that, in this system of co-ordinates, the point where politics and simple human morality intersect is only idealism.

Raisa M Gorbachev (1932-), Russian
political figure and partner to former
Premier Mikhail Gorbachev

Changing of the guard at the presidential palace in Brasilia, Brazil.

When spite is shoving you forward,
making your own soul a hypocrite,
towards the disgrace of a shot
or a word —
don't hurry, don't do it!

**Stop, O people of the Earth as you run
so blindly to the next assault!
bullet, freeze as you fly from the gun,
and you, bomb in mid-air, halt!**

Yevgeny Yevtushenko (1933-), Russian poet

WE ARE GOING TO KEEP WATCH over the lands of our country so that they truly profit her children. We are going to restore ancient laws and make new ones which will be just and noble. We are going to put an end to suppression of free thought and see to it that all our citizens enjoy to the full the fundamental liberties foreseen in the Declaration of Human Rights. We are going to do away with all discrimination of every variety and assure for each and all the position to which human dignity, work and dedication entitles them. We are going to rule not by the peace of guns and bayonets but by a peace of the heart and the will.

Patrice Lumumba (1925-1961), assassinated independence leader and first Prime Minister of the Congo, from his Independence Day speech in 1960. He is pictured arriving in Belgium for a conference in the same year.

You cannot shake hands
with a clenched fist.

Indira Gandhi (1917-1984), Indian prime minister

**WHAT CAN YOU DO BY
KILLING? NOTHING. YOU
KILL ONE DOG, THE MASTER
BUYS ANOTHER – THAT'S ALL
THERE IS TO IT.**

Maxim Gorky (1868-1936), Russian novelist and playwright

I HATE IT when they say, 'He gave his life for his country'. Nobody gives their life for anything. We steal the lives of these kids. We take it away from them. They don't die for the honour and glory of their country. We kill them.

Gene LaRoque (1917-), US Admiral and, later, dissident

A child soldier in the Sudan People's Liberation Army, pictured near the village of Boeth, southern Sudan.

Peace is not an absence of war, it is a virtue, a state of mind, a disposition for benevolence, confidence, justice.

Baruch Spinoza (1632-1677), rationalist Dutch philosopher

A peace education class in post-war Afghanistan.

83

Look here, that's the right way
to look History
in the face, not like you: in the
crude irresponsible fragments,
the sniper shot that penetrates
deep into the skull,
the graves already covered over
by irredeemable grass

Ferida Durakovic (1957-), Bosnian poet

A graveyard in Sarajevo, Bosnia-Herzegovina, during the 1992-1995 civil war.

Since wars begin in the minds of people,

Women in Burundi help launch the Back to School campaign in October 2004.

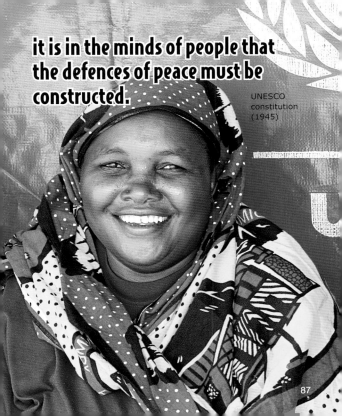

it is in the minds of people that the defences of peace must be constructed.

UNESCO constitution (1945)

87

All war must be just the killing of strangers against whom you feel no personal animosity; strangers whom, in other circumstances, you would help if you found them in trouble, and who would help you if you needed it.

Mark Twain (Sam Clemens) 1835-1910, US writer

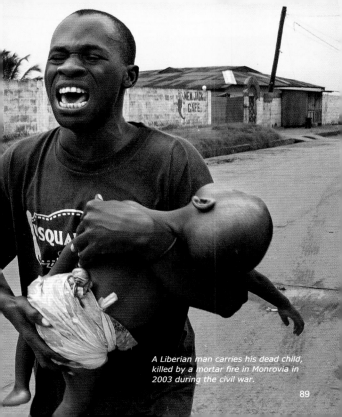

A Liberian man carries his dead child, killed by a mortar fire in Monrovia in 2003 during the civil war.

89

PEA

A demonstration in Istanbul, Turkey, against the war in Iraq. The posters say 'Don't come Bush', referring to the US President's imminent visit for a NATO summit.

ZULME
KARŞI
DİRENECEĞİZ
Yaşasın
Küresel
Yaşasın
Küresel
İntifa
GELME
BUSH
GELME
BUSH

Weapons being burned as part of the Disarmament, Demobilization, Rehabilitation and Reintegration process in Burundi in December 2004.

THE PEACE we seek, founded upon decent trust and co-operative effort among nations, can be fortified, not by weapons of war but by wheat and by cotton, by milk and by wool, by meat and by timber and by rice. These are words that translate into every language on earth. These are needs that challenge this world in arms.

Dwight D Eisenhower (1890-1969), US President and General

93

Peace is achieved one person at a time, through a series of friendships.

Fatma Reda (contemporary), Egyptian-born US psychiatrist

A Portuguese UN peacekeeper accompanied by local children in the Becora district of Dili, Timor-Leste, in March 2000.

AND JOY IS EVERYWHERE; it is in the earth's green covering of grass; in the blue serenity of the sky; in the reckless exuberance of spring; in the serene abstinence of grey winter; in the living flesh that animates our bodily frame; in the perfect poise of the human figure, noble and upright; in living; in the exercise of all our powers; in the acquisition of knowledge.

Rabindranath Tagore (1861-1941), Indian poet

Put away the book, the description, the tradition, the authority, and take the journey of self-discovery. Love, and don't be caught in opinions and ideas about what love is or should be. When you love, everything will come right. Love has its own action. Love, and you will know the blessings of it. Keep away from the authority who tells you what love is and what it is not. No authority knows and he who knows cannot tell. Love, and there is understanding.

Jiddu Krishnamurthy (1895-1986), Indian philosopher

THE ARMY HANDS OVER THE KEYS TO THE BARRACKS, TO BE CONVERTED INTO A CULTURAL CENTRE... WE ARE THE SUSTAINERS OF A NEW WORLD IN AMERICA. LITTLE COSTA RICA OFFERS ITS HEART AND LOVE TO CIVILIAN RULE AND DEMOCRACY.

José Figueres, President of Costa Rica, on 1 December 1948 when he abolished the army at a stroke. To this day, the Central American nation has no army. It has instead devoted its resources to healthcare and education. It is no coincidence that it has the lowest infant mortality rate in Latin America outside Cuba.

101

For a Nuclear Free and Independent Pacific

If the recognized leaders of humankind who have control over the engines of destruction were wholly to renounce their use, with full knowledge of its implications, permanent peace could be obtained. This is clearly impossible without the Great Powers of the earth renouncing their imperialistic design. This, again, seems impossible without great nations ceasing to believe in soul-destroying competition and to desire to multiply wants and, therefore, increase their material possessions.

Mohandas Karamchand Gandhi (1869-1948), leader of India's freedom movement

The army on patrol near Guazapa mountain, El Salvador, during the 1980-1992 civil war.

PEACE IN GUATEMALA
is not a myth, neither
is it a myth for Central
America, or for the people
of this continent or other
continents. Rather, it is
a process which requires
effort and consciousness-
raising around the world,
especially among those
in governments and in
large organizations who
have the power to make
important decisions.

Rigoberta Menchú Tum (1959-), Guatemalan
activist for indigenous rights, and Nobel Peace
Prize winner, 1992

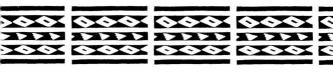

THE NINE PRECEPTS of the
Code of Right Relationship:

1 Speak only words of truth.

2 Speak only of the good qualities of others.

3 Be confident and carry no tales.

4 Turn aside the veil of anger to release the beauty inherent in all.

5 Waste not the bounty, and want not.

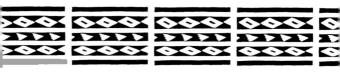

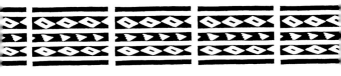

6 Honour the light in all. Compare nothing; see all for its suchness.

7 Respect all life; cut away ignorance from one's own heart.

8 Neither kill nor harbour thoughts of angry nature, which destroy peace like an arrow.

9 Do it now; if you see what needs doing, do it.

Dhyani Ywahoo (contemporary), Cherokee Nation

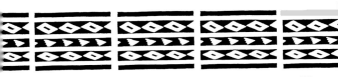

Peace, n.
In international affairs, a period of cheating between two periods of fighting.

Ambrose Bierce (1842-1914), US writer and journalist

WHEN IT'S A QUESTION OF PEACE ONE MUST TALK TO THE DEVIL HIMSELF.

Édouard Herriot (1872-1957), French politician

IT SEEMS that once an initial judgement has been made that a war is just, there is a tendency to stop thinking, to assume then that everything done on behalf of victory is morally acceptable. I had myself participated in the bombing of cities, without even considering whether there was

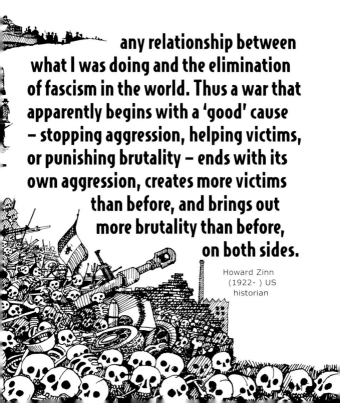

any relationship between what I was doing and the elimination of fascism in the world. Thus a war that apparently begins with a 'good' cause – stopping aggression, helping victims, or punishing brutality – ends with its own aggression, creates more victims than before, and brings out more brutality than before, on both sides.

Howard Zinn
(1922-) US
historian

Cost of three B2-Spirit Stealth bombers at $2.2 billion each = $6.6 BILLION

Extra annual cost above current spending of achieving primary education for ALL worldwide by 2015 = $5.6 BILLION

'Salaam'
'Peace'

The daily greeting in Arabic

'Shalom'
'Peace'

The daily greeting in Hebrew

116

DRIVEN BY THE FORCES OF LOVE, THE FRAGMENTS OF THE WORLD SEEK EACH OTHER SO THAT THE WORLD MAY COME TO BEING.

Pierre Teilhard de Chardin (1881-1955), French Jesuit theologian, palaeontologist and philosopher

Serb women grieving
for lost family members
in Gorazdevic, Kosovo,
during the NATO bombing
campaign in 1999.

The Kosovo bombing was unique not because it was styled 'humanitarian' but because it was the first-ever major conflict with no military casualties at all on the winning side – absolute impunity made manifest, and a truly terrifying prospect.

David Rap... ... (1946) English journalist

ARE WE SEEKING POWER FOR POWER'S SAKE?
Or are we seeking to make the world and our nation better places to live? If we seek the latter, violence can never provide the answer. The ultimate weakness of violence is that it is a descending spiral, begetting the very thing it seeks to destroy. Instead of diminishing evil, it multiplies it. Through violence you may murder the liar, but you cannot murder the lie, nor establish the truth. Through violence you may murder the hater, but you do not murder hate. In fact, violence merely increases hate. So it goes. Returning violence for violence multiplies violence, adding deeper darkness to a night already devoid of stars. Darkness cannot drive out hate; only love can do that.

Martin Luther King Jr (1929-1968), African-American leader

On 15 February 2003 the biggest demonstration in British history took place in London opposing the imminent war on Iraq (pictured left).

There were more than 600 demonstrations on that day in cities on every continent including: Adelaide, Albacete, Alicante, Amsterdam, Athens, Auckland, Bangkok, Barcelona, Beirut, Belfast, Berlin, Berne, Brisbane, Brussels, Budapest, Busan, Cairo, Calgary, Canberra, Cape Town, Chicago, Chittagong, Copenhagen, Cyprus British Army Bases, Damascus, Dhaka, Dili, Dublin, Edmonton, Foster, Geelong, Glasgow, Granada, Guernsey, Havana, Helsinki, Hobart, Hong Kong, Huelva, Islamabad, Istanbul, Jaén, Jakarta, Jersey, Johannesburg, Kiev, Kigali, Kuala Lumpur, Lahore, Launceston, Lisbon, Lismore, Ljubljana, London, Los Angeles, Luxembourg, Madrid, Málaga, Manila, Martinique, Melbourne, Mexico City, Montreal, Moscow, Murcia, New York, Newcastle [Australia], Osaka, Oslo, Oviedo, Paris, Perth, Philadelphia, Poznan, Prague, Ramallah, Reunion Island, Reykjavik, Rockhampton, Rome, Salamanca, San Francisco, San Juan, Santander, Santo Domingo, Sao Paulo, Seattle, Seoul, Shetlands, Skopje, Sofia, Stockholm, Strahan, Sydney, Takaka, Tallinn, Tel Aviv, Tokyo, Toronto, Vienna, Valletta, Vigo, Vilnius, Warsaw, Wollongong.

A peace-maker often receives wounds.

Yoruba proverb (Benin, Nigeria, Togo)

BETTER KEEP PEACE THAN MAKE PEACE.

Dutch proverb

When a person finds no peace within themselves, it is useless to seek it elsewhere.

French proverb

A man with outward courage dares to die
A man with inward courage dares to live.

Lao-Tzu (c 600 BCE), Taoist sage, Chinese proverb

I will not die an
unlived life,
I will not go in fear
Of falling or catching
fire.
I choose to inhabit
my days,
To allow my living to
open to me,
To make me less afraid,
More accessible,
To loosen my heart
Until it becomes a wing
A torch, a promise.

Dawna Markova (contemporary),
US academic and author

PEACE IS MORE FATTENING THAN FOOD.

Ovambo proverb
(Angola, Namibia)

It is better to build bridges than walls.

Swahili proverb (East Africa)

IN REMEMBRANCE OF ALL THE WOMEN WHO WERE RAPED AND MURDERED BY MEN AT WAR
OUR TEARS ARE FOR THEM TODAY

A wreath placed on the fence at Greenham Common US airbase in England, December 1982.

I see little hope for a peaceful world until men are excluded from the realm of foreign policy altogether and all decisions concerning international relations are reserved for women, preferably married ones.

WH Auden (1907-1973), English poet

Reply not roughly to smooth language, nor Contend with him who knocks at peace's door.

Sheikh Sadi, 13th century Persian Sufi poet

The world is wide for those who
live in peace, narrow for
those who quarrel.

Uzbek proverb

Make peace with people and quarrel with your sins.

Russian proverb

Peace pays what war gains.

Serbo-Croat proverb

One word, one action, or one thought can reduce another person's suffering and bring them joy. One word can give comfort and confidence, destroy doubt, help someone avoid a mistake, reconcile a conflict, or open the door to liberation. One action can save a person's life or help them take advantage of a rare opportunity. One thought can do the same, because thoughts always lead to words and actions. If love is in our heart, every thought, word and deed can bring about a miracle.

Thich Nhat Hanh (1926-), Vietnamese
Buddhist monk and peace practitioner

Sandino sunrise... The young Augusto Cesar Sandino, the iconic rebel leader who gave his name to the Sandinista movement in Nicaragua.

My personal revenge will be to tell you
Good morning
On a street without beggars or homeless
When instead of jailing you I suggest
You shake away the sadness there that
blinds you
And when you have applied your hands
in torture
Are unable to look up at what
surrounds you
My personal revenge will be to give you
These hands that once you so mistreated
But have failed to take away their
tenderness.

Tomás Borge (1930-), Nicaraguan poet. As Justice Minister in
the revolutionary Sandinista government during the 1980s, Borge
put his principles into practice by operating humane 'open-prison'
regimes for former members of the dictator Somoza's National
Guard who had tortured him and killed his wife.

You'll never have a quiet world until you knock the patriotism out of the human race.

George Bernard Shaw (1856-1950), Irish dramatist

WE STAND HERE today as nothing more than a representative of the millions of our people who dared to rise up against a social system whose very essence is war, violence, racism, oppression, repression and the impoverishment of an entire people.

Nelson Mandela (1918-), first President of democratic South Africa, pictured voting for the first time in 1994

OUR PEOPLE are peace-loving to a fault. The response of the authorities has been an escalating intransigence and violence, the violence of police dogs, tear gas, detention without trial, exile, and even death.

Desmond Tutu (1931-), South African Archbishop, from his Nobel Peace Prize acceptance speech in 1984

USING TREES as a symbol
of peace is in keeping
with a widespread
African tradition. Many
communities in Africa have
these traditions.

For example, the elders of the Kikuyu carried a staff from the thigi tree that, when placed between two disputing sides, caused them to stop fighting and seek reconciliation.

Wangari Maathai (1940-), founder of tree-planting Greenbelt Movement, Kenya, Nobel Peace Prize 2004, acceptance lecture

I am an uncompromising pacifist... I have no sense of nationalism, only a cosmic consciousness of belonging to the human family.

Rosika Schwimer (1877-1948),
Hungarian writer, editor,
pacifist, suffragist

149

Cost of producing one landmine = $3
Cost of clearing one landmine = $1,000

**Over 200 million landmines are stockpiled
in the arsenals of 78 countries**

**Landmines still claim between 15,000
and 20,000 new victims each year, many
of them in countries no longer in conflict.
Over 80 per cent of the victims are
civilians and nearly one-third are children.**

BUT
Since the Mine Ban Treaty was concluded in 1997, thanks to a massive worldwide popular campaign by activists and NGOs, 152 governments have signed the treaty and 144 of those have formally ratified it.

Since the International Campaign to Ban Landmines began its work, the number of mine-producing countries has dropped from over 50 in 1992 to 15 as of 2004.

Source: International Campaign to Ban Landmines

151

We need to abolish the word 'enemy'.

It is fear that creates enemies.

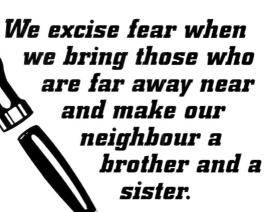

We excise fear when we bring those who are far away near and make our neighbour a brother and a sister.

Leonardo Boff (1938-),
Brazilian liberation
theologian

ENE MY!

153

British Army firing squad, c 1855.

I have never seen anyone morally improved by killing; neither the one who aimed the bullet, nor the one who received it in the flesh.

Daniel Berrigan (1921-),
radical US Catholic priest

To be able to pull the trigger and kill someone you have to block off what is human about them – it helps the firing squad as well as the victim if a blindfold covers the eyes.

Chris Brazier (1955-),
English journalist

'How can we determine the hour of dawn, when the night ends and the day begins?' asked the Teacher. 'When from a distance you can distinguish between a dog and a sheep,' suggested one of the students.

'No,' was the answer.

'Is it when one can distinguish between a fig tree and a grapevine?' asked a

156

second student.
'No.'
'Please tell us the answer,
then.'
'It is when you can look in
the face of another human
being and you have enough
light to recognize in them
your brother or your sister.
Until then it is night and
darkness is still with us.'

Hasidic proverb

True peace is not merely the absence of tension: it is the presence of justice.

Martin Luther King Jr (1929-1968), assassinated
African-American leader

YOU CAN'T SEPARATE PEACE FROM FREEDOM BECAUSE NO ONE CAN BE AT PEACE UNLESS THEY HAVE THEIR FREEDOM.

Malcolm X (1925-1965), assassinated
African-American leader

True peace is not merely the absence of tension: it is the presence of justice.

Martin Luther King Jr (1929-1968), assassinated
African-American leader

YOU CAN'T SEPARATE PEACE FROM FREEDOM BECAUSE NO ONE CAN BE AT PEACE UNLESS THEY HAVE THEIR FREEDOM.

Malcolm X (1925-1965), assassinated
African-American leader

Brothers, you came from our own people. You are killing your own brothers. Any human order to kill must be subordinate to the law of God, which says, 'THOU SHALT NOT KILL'. No soldier is obliged to obey an order contrary to the law of God.

Archbishop Oscar Romero (1917-1980), assassinated in El Salvador

STRIKE AGAINST WAR, for without you no battles can be fought! Strike against manufacturing shrapnel and gas bombs and all other tools of murder! Strike against preparedness that means death and misery to millions of human beings! Be not dumb, obedient slaves in an army of destruction! Be heroes in an army of construction!

Helen Keller (1880-1968), US deafblind activist and socialist

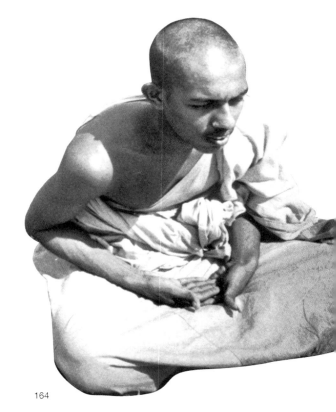

Hatreds never cease through hatreds in this world. Through love alone they cease. This is an eternal law.

Gautama Buddha (563-483 BCE), from the Dhammapada

I hold myself incapable of hating any being on earth. By a long course of prayerful discipline, I have ceased over 40 years to hate anybody. I know this is a big claim. Nevertheless, I make it in all humility.

Mohandas Karamchand Gandhi (1869-1948), leader of India's freedom movement

Together we can stop the bomb

OUR QUEST for peace must start with the recognition that the roots of unpeaceful relationships often lie, deep and unacknowledged, within ourselves. Only if we start from this reluctant recognition will we be able to break our suicide pact with the Bomb and become real peacemakers.

Glen Williams (1944-), Australian journalist

I AM IMMENSELY and continuously conscious of a world of nuclear bombs, of vast hunger, of curable injustice, of a meretricious press and cheapjack television, of perilous and apparently endless international division, of unreasonable cruelty and suffering for which almost nobody cares, and of my own silly efforts to make money to provide me with irrelevant comforts or necessities like drink and to ensure some measure of security for my family. And I know that it is not the answer, because there is

truthfully only one answer, which is absolute pacifism and absolute communism
– not in the dreary dogmatic party-political sense, but in the sense that my father would have called religious: the sense of moral community. Not only do I know it; I knew it all along.

James Cameron
(1911-1985),
British journalist

**MAY THE SPIRIT BLESS YOU WITH DISCOMFORT
AT EASY ANSWERS, HALF-TRUTHS AND SUPERFICIAL RELATIONSHIPS SO THAT YOU WILL LIVE DEEP IN YOUR HEART.**

**AND MAY THE SPIRIT BLESS YOU WITH THE FOOLISHNESS
TO THINK YOU CAN MAKE THE DIFFERENCE
IN THE WORLD, SO THAT YOU WILL DO THE THINGS
WHICH OTHERS SAY CANNOT BE DONE.**

Interfaith Council for Peace and Justice, Ann Arbor, Michigan

NOT PEACE AT ANY PRICE, BUT LOVE AT ALL COSTS.

Dick Sheppard (1880-1937),
British founder
of the Peace
Pledge Union

THERE IS A WAY TO PEACE.
PEACE IS THE WAY.

AJ Muste (1885-1967), US pacifist

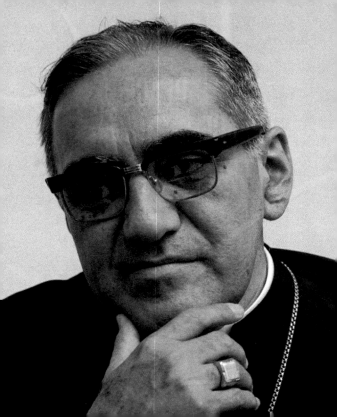

PEACE is not the product of terror or fear. Peace is not the silence of cemeteries. Peace is not the silent result of violent repression. Peace is the generous, tranquil contribution of all to the good of all. Peace is dynamism. Peace is generosity. It is right and it is duty.

El Salvador's assassinated Archbishop Oscar Romero (1917-1980), pictured left

THE MILITARY IS A ROLE MODEL FOR THE BUSINESS WORLD.

Robert Dilenschneider, ex-CEO,
Hill & Knowlton, US PR company

177

This is war, then: All is well.
The missiles bomb the cities,
and the airplanes bid the clouds
farewell.
It is nothing but a corpse which
grows and stretches
Between Kirkuk and Isfahan,
Between Baghdad and Qum,
Between Irbil and Tehran,
Between time and time,
Between blood and blood.
All is well. Except for this spring
approaching from afar,
Except for these birds flying between
one front and another,
Except for those who await their death in
silence,
Except for this mother whose cries I can
hear from afar.
Ah! I saw eyes glowing amidst

the branches,
A monster running on a sea-coast
Gliding down from my heart.
Peace to you, O Iraq!
Peace to springtime, coming
forth from the fissures of the
earth!
Peace to Baghdad, redeemer
and redeemed!
Peace to Basra, to its burnt
palm-trees!
Peace to Kirkuk, to its red sky!
Peace to Amara, to its marshes
mined with dynamite!
Peace to the fourteen provinces!
Thus does the war get up from sleep.
A man takes it to a hillock
And leaves it in History.

Fadhil al-Azzawi (1940-), Iraqi poet now living in Germany, from
the poem 'Every Morning The War Gets Up From Sleep'

Better a lean peace than a fat victory.

English proverb

In peace do not forget war.

Japanese proverb

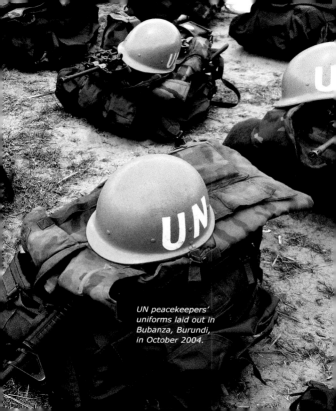

UN peacekeepers'
uniforms laid out in
Bubanza, Burundi,
in October 2004.

You must have been taught – and I was taught – that peace is the opposite of war. But is it? In India, peace is a daily battle for food and shelter and dignity. We need much more to understand what's wrong with peace than to understand why we go to war. Once you're at war, all the logic is gone. You can't ask any questions any more. For people, especially people in the media, it's very important to understand that wars are also very marketable. So you spend a lot more time – wars are given a lot more space than a flawed peace. Whereas if that were not the case, and you were to spend more time in the real flaws in the so-called peace, you might be able to avert war.

Arundhati Roy (1961-), Indian writer and activist

Times Square, New York, 1969 – one of 11 billboards in major world cities purchased by John Lennon and Yoko Ono to display their peace message.

The Blue Meanies, or whatever they are, still preach violence all the time in every newspaper, every TV show and every magazine. The least Yoko and I can do is hog the headlines and make people laugh. We're quite willing to be the world's clowns if it will do any good. For reasons known only to themselves, people print what I say. And I say 'peace'.

John Lennon (1940-1980), British rock musician and former Beatle

JUST SOME OF THE MANY PEACE-RELATED CAMPAIGNING ORGANIZATIONS...

INTERNATIONAL

Abolition 2000 c/o Pax Christi USA, 532 W 8th Street, Erie, PA 16502, US.
tel: +1 814 453 4955 email: admin@abolition2000.org
web: www.abolition2000.org

Codepink – Women for Peace, 2010 Linden Ave, Venice, CA, 90291, US.
tel: +1 310 827 4320
email: info@codepinkalert.org
web: www.codepink4peace.org

Hague Appeal for Peace
tel: +1 212 687 2623
email: hap@haguepeace.org
web: www.haguepeace.org

Pax Christi International
Rue du Vieux Marché aux Grains 21, B-1000, Brussels, Belgium.
tel: +32 2 502 55 50 email: webmaster@paxchristi.net
web: www.paxchristi.net

Peace Brigades International The Grayston Centre, 28 Charles Square, London N1 6HT, England. tel: +44-20 7324 4628 email: info@peacebrigades.org
web: www.peacebrigades.org

Women's International League for Peace and Freedom
Geneva Secretariat, 1 rue de Varambe, 1211 Geneva, Switzerland.
tel: +41 22 919 7080
email: wilpf@iprolink.ch
United Nations Office, 777 UN Plaza, New York, NY 10017. tel: +1 212 682 1265 email: info@reaching criticalwill.org web: www. reachingcriticalwill.org

AUSTRALIA

Anti-Nuclear Alliance of Western Australia
email: admin@anawa.org.au
web: www.anawa.org
Australian Anti-Bases Campaign Coalition
PO Box A899, Sydney South,

NSW 1235499.
tel: 02 9698 2954.
email: aabcc@zipworld.com.au
web: www.anti-bases.org

Australian Peace Committee www.peacecourier.com/

International Peace Pilgrimage toward a nuclear free future web: www.violet.com.au/html/index.php

Medical Association for Prevention of War
web: www.mapw.org.au

Nuclear Free Australia
PO Box 1044 Upwey 3158.
tel: 0417 506 150 email:
nukefreeaus@green.net.au
web: www.nukefreeaus.org

Nowar SA 239 Wright Street, Adelaide, 5000. tel: 0414 773 918. web: www.nowar-sa.net

Sydney Peace and Justice Coalition
web: www.nswpeace.org

Victorian Peace Network
Suite 2, Victorian Trades Hall Council, 54 Victoria Street, Carlton South 3053. tel: 03 9659 3582. web: www.vicpeace.org

BRITAIN

Peace Pledge Union 1 Peace Passage, London N7 0BT.
tel: 020 7424 9444
web: www.ppu.org.uk

Campaign for Nuclear Disarmament 162 Holloway Road, London N7 8DQ.
tel: 020 7700 2393
email: enquiries@cnduk.org
web: www.cnduk.org

Campaign Against Arms Trade 11 Goodwin St, London N4 3HQ. tel: 020 7281 0297.
web: www.caat.org.uk

Our World Our Say Suite 5A, 68 Middle St, Brighton BN1 1AL. tel: 01273 201318 email: info@ourworldoursay.org
web: www.ourworldoursay.org

Stop the War Coalition
27 Britannia Street, London WC1X 9JP. Tel: 020 7278 6694/07951 593525
email: office@stopwar.org.uk
web: www.StopWar.org.uk

Trident Ploughshares 2000
42-46 Bethel St, Norwich NR2 1NR. tel: 0845 45 88 366
web: www.gn.apc.org/tp2000

CANADA
Canadian Peace Alliance
427 Bloor St W, Box 13, Toronto, ON, M5S 1X7. tel: 416 588 5555
email: cpa@web.ca
web: http://www.acp-cpa.ca/en/index.htm
Canadian Network to Abolish Nuclear Weapons
145 Spruce St, Suite 208, Ottawa, Ontario, Canada, K1R 6P1. tel: 613 233 1982
email: cnanw@web.ca
web: www.web.net/~cnanw/
Canadian Voice of Women for Peace
761 Queen St. W. #203, Toronto, ON. M6J 1G1. tel: 416 603 7915 email: vow@ca.inter.net web: http://home.ca.inter.net/~vow/
Coalition to Oppose the Arms Trade
541 McLeod St, Ottawa, ON, K1R 5R2. tel: 613 231 3076
web: http://coat.ncf.ca/
Conscience Canada
901-70 Mill St, Toronto, ON, M5A 4R1. tel: 416 203 1402 email:

consciencecanada@shaw.ca
web: http://members.shaw.ca/consciencecanada/
Nonviolent Peace Force
211 Bronson Avenue, Suite 309A, Ottawa, ON, K1R 6H5. tel: 613 564 0999
email: info@npcanada.org
web: www.npcanada.org
Project Ploughshares
57 Erb Street, West Waterloo, ON, N2L 6C2. tel: 519 888 6541
web: www.ploughshares.ca
War Resisters Support Campaign
Box 13, 427 Bloor Street W, Toronto, ON, M5S 1X7. tel: 416 598 1222
email: resisters@sympatico.ca
web: www.resisters.ca

IRELAND
Irish CND
PO Box 6327, Dublin 6. tel: 01 836 7264
email: irishcnd@ireland.com
web: http://indigo.ie/~goodwill/icnd.html

NEW ZEALAND/ AOTEAROA
Campaign Against Foreign Control of Aotearoa
email: cafca@chch.planet.

org.nz web: http://
canterbury.cyberplace.org.
nz/community/CAFCA
Global Peace and Justice
Auckland Private Bag 68905,
Newton, Auckland.
web: http://gpja.pl.net
Peace Movement Aotearoa
PO Box 9314, Wellington.
tel: 04 382 8129
email: pma@apc.org.nz web:
www.converge.org.nz/pma

UNITED STATES
Global Coalition for Peace
4209 East-West Highway,
Chevy Chase, Maryland
20815. tel: 301 654 4899
email: peaceseekers@globa
lcoalitionforpeace.net web:
http://home.earthlink.
net/~coalition4peace/
**Institute for Peace and
Justice** 4144 Lindell
Boulevard #408, St Louis,
MO 63108, tel: 314 533 4445
email: ppjn@aol.com web:
www.ipj-ppj.org
**National Grassroots Peace
Network**/endthewar.org PO
Box 60428, Washington, DC

20039. tel 301 270 4858
**National War Tax
Resistance** Coordinating
Committee PO Box 150553,
Brooklyn, NY 11215. email:
nwtrcc@nwtrcc.org web:
www.nwtrcc.org
**Nuclear Age Peace
Foundation** 1187 Coast
Village Road, Suite 1, PMB 121,
Santa Barbara, CA 93108-
2794. tel: 805 965 3443
web: www.wagingpeace.org
United for Peace & Justice
PO Box 607, Times Square
Station, New York, NY 10108.
tel: 212 868 5545
web: www.unitedforpeace.org
**Vietnam Veterans Against
the War** PO Box 408594,
Chicago, IL 60640. tel: 773
276 4189 email: vvaw@vvaw.
org web: www.vvaw.org
War Resisters League 339
Lafayette St, New York, NY
10012. tel: 212 228 0450
email: wrl@warresisters.org
web: www.warresisters.org

More wit, wisdom and inspiration from the New Internationalist BOOKS TO GO...

'The highest expression of dignity can be summed up in the single word "No!" – being able to say "No!" when you disagree.'

Dai Qing (contemporary), Chinese journalist and campaigner against China's Three Gorges Dam project

'If you think you are too small to make a difference, try sleeping with a mosquito.'

Tensing Gyatso (1935-), current Tibetan Dalai Lama

ORDER ONLINE AT: www.newint.org/shop

New Internationalist Publications is a co-operative with offices in Oxford (England), Adelaide (Australia), Toronto (Canada) and Christchurch (New Zealand/Aotearoa). It exists to report on the issues of world poverty and inequality; to focus attention on the unjust relationship between the powerful and powerless in both rich and poor nations; to debate and campaign for the radical changes necessary within and between those nations if the basic material and spiritual needs of all are to be met; and to bring to life the people, the ideas, the action in the fight for global justice.

The monthly **New Internationalist** magazine now has more than 75,000 subscribers worldwide. In addition to the magazine, the co-operative publishes the One World Calendar and the One World Almanac, outstanding collections of full-colour photographs. It also publishes books, including: the successful series of No–Nonsense Guides to the key issues in the world today; cookbooks containing recipes and cultural information from around the world; and photographic books on topics such as Nomadic Peoples and Water. The **NI** is the English-language publisher of the biennial reference book *The World Guide*, written by the Instituto del Tercer Mundo in Uruguay.

The co-operative is financially independent but aims to break even; any surpluses are reinvested so as to bring New Internationalist publications to as many people as possible.

www.newint.org